Opening up
Oba

GW00585502

ANDREW THOMSON

DayOne

ALSO BY ANDREW THOMSON ...

Opening up
Deuteronomy

ANDREW THOMSON

Commendations for *Opening up
Deuteronomy*:

This commentary ...
is perceptive in its
comments, lively in
style and most helpful
in relating the teaching
of the book to the overall theology of
the Bible. Bible students and preachers
will find it stimulating. I will be
recommending it warmly.

Allan M. Harman, former Principal and Professor of Old
Testament, Presbyterian Theological College, Melbourne,
Australia, and author of *Deuteronomy: The Commands of
a Covenant God* (Christian Focus, 2001).

Crisp, clear and contemporary. For any
who wish to delve into Deuteronomy
either as a group or for private study,
this is just right.

Brian Edwards, Christian minister, author and editor

© Day One Publications 2016

First printed 2016

All Scripture quotations, unless stated otherwise, are from the anglicized edition of
the ESV Bible copyright © 2002 Collins, part of HarperCollins Publishers.

ISBN 978-1-84625-552-6

British Library Cataloguing in Publication Data available
Published by Day One Publications
Ryelands Road, Leominster, England, HR6 8NZ
Telephone 01568 613 740   FAX 01568 611 473
email—sales@dayone.co.uk
web site—www.dayone.co.uk

Printed by TJ International

*This book is sent out to the glory of the God
who cares for his people,
with the prayer that all readers might increasingly
'possess their possessions' and 'seek first the kingdom
of God'.*

List of Bible abbreviations

THE OLD TESTAMENT		1 Chr.	1 Chronicles	Dan.	Daniel
		2 Chr.	2 Chronicles	Hosea	Hosea
Gen.	Genesis	Ezra	Ezra	Joel	Joel
Exod.	Exodus	Neh.	Nehemiah	Amos	Amos
Lev.	Leviticus	Esth.	Esther	Obad.	Obadiah
Num.	Numbers	Job	Job	Jonah	Jonah
Deut.	Deuteronomy	Ps.	Psalms	Micah	Micah
Josh.	Joshua	Prov.	Proverbs	Nahum	Nahum
Judg.	Judges	Eccles.	Ecclesiastes	Hab.	Habakkuk
Ruth	Ruth	S.of S.	Song of Solomon	Zeph.	Zephaniah
1 Sam.	1 Samuel	Isa.	Isaiah	Hag.	Haggai
2 Sam.	2 Samuel	Jer.	Jeremiah	Zech.	Zechariah
1 Kings	1 Kings	Lam.	Lamentations	Mal.	Malachi
2 Kings	2 Kings	Ezek.	Ezekiel		

THE NEW TESTAMENT		Gal.	Galatians	Heb.	Hebrews
		Eph.	Ephesians	James	James
Matt.	Matthew	Phil.	Philippians	1 Peter	1 Peter
Mark	Mark	Col.	Colossians	2 Peter	2 Peter
Luke	Luke	1 Thes.	1 Thessalonians	1 John	1 John
John	John	2 Thes.	2 Thessalonians	2 John	2 John
Acts	Acts	1 Tim.	1 Timothy	3 John	3 John
Rom.	Romans	2 Tim.	2 Timothy	Jude	Jude
1 Cor.	1 Corinthians	Titus	Titus	Rev.	Revelation
2 Cor.	2 Corinthians	Philem.	Philemon		

Contents

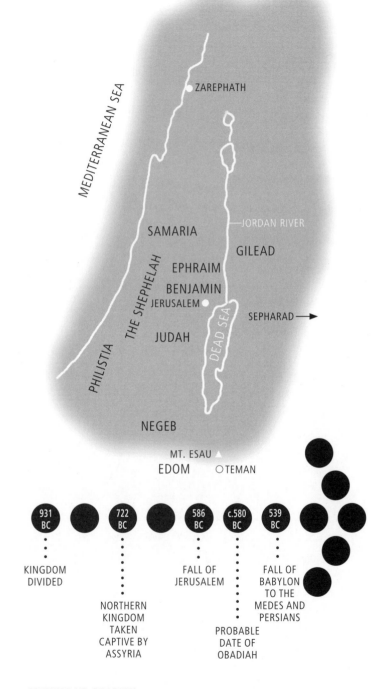

MEDITERRANEAN SEA

ZAREPHATH

JORDAN RIVER

SAMARIA

GILEAD

THE SHEPHELAH

EPHRAIM

BENJAMIN

JERUSALEM

SEPHARAD ⟶

PHILISTIA

JUDAH

DEAD SEA

NEGEB

MT. ESAU ▲

EDOM   ○ TEMAN

931 BC		722 BC		586 BC	c.580 BC	539 BC		
KINGDOM DIVIDED				FALL OF JERUSALEM		FALL OF BABYLON TO THE MEDES AND PERSIANS		
		NORTHERN KINGDOM TAKEN CAPTIVE BY ASSYRIA			PROBABLE DATE OF OBADIAH			

OPENING UP OBADIAH

1 Introduction
(v. 1)

To understand what the Lord has to say 'concerning Edom' we'll need to concern ourselves with the history of one of Israel's oldest enemies. Little do they know that the surrounding nations are already planning their downfall.

Concerning the author

We know hardly anything about Obadiah, and perhaps that is as it should be for someone whose name means 'servant of the LORD'. It is the message and the master that really matter. We come across a number of other Obadiahs in the Bible but it is unlikely that any of them are the author of this book. Our Obadiah would no doubt subscribe to John the Baptist's conviction: 'He must increase, but I must decrease' (John 3:30)—or, as George Whitefield put it, 'Let the name of George Whitefield perish so long as Christ is exalted!'[1]

Concerning the date

We are also uncertain about the date of Obadiah's prophecy.

We know that it refers to a 'day of calamity' for Jerusalem, but exactly which one is not so clear. Looking at parallel passages in Jeremiah (49:7–22), Lamentations (4:18–22) and Ezekiel (25:12–14; ch. 35), the similarities suggest that the fall of Jerusalem in 586 BC is being referred to, placing the date of the prophecy shortly after that.

> While it concerns Edom, the prophecy is really designed for the encouragement of God's people.

Prophets didn't often address towns and nations beyond Israel. There are sections in the major prophets (Isa. 13–23; Jer. 46–51; Ezek. 25–32) but only two books that focus on the fate of Israel's enemies. Nahum's oracle concerns Nineveh and Obadiah's vision concerns Edom. There is no record of Obadiah's prophecy having been delivered to the people of Edom. It looks very much as if, while it concerns Edom, the prophecy is really designed for the encouragement of God's people.

Concerning Edom's past

We might not know much about the date and author, but we know plenty about Edom. Genesis 36:8 alerts us to the fact that 'Esau is Edom'. The nation of Edom was descended from Jacob's twin brother, Esau. The relationship between the two brothers and their offspring had never been straightforward. The struggle between Jacob and Esau began before they were even born. Even then Rebekah was told that it was a contest that would ultimately be between not just brothers but nations (Gen. 25:23). Jacob proved himself an opportunist when it came to procuring the birthright, but went a significant step further when it came to securing his father's blessing. The cry of 'cheat!' was justified, and it gave birth to a hatred that was nursed for years. Hatred on the one side bred fear on the other, and, despite an uneasy truce, Jacob and Esau were never properly reconciled.

The two families went their separate ways for a good while, developing (as promised; see Gen. 25:23) into nations in their own right. Next time we come across Edom the shoe is on the other foot: it is Edom's turn to fear. We read of its chiefs being 'dismayed' (Exod. 15:15) by news of Israel's Red Sea crossing, clearly concerned that they might be next on the receiving end of the Lord's 'glorious deeds' (Exod. 15:11). Their concern, however, did nothing to soften their attitude to Israel. Not all that long afterwards Moses' request to be allowed to pass through their land was given short shrift. His appeal was respectful, reminding them of their shared ancestry, promising not to damage crops or water supplies, and also offering compensation. This was met with a blunt refusal, reinforced by an intimidating show of force. The message was clear: the family feud had not been forgotten. But then the Lord would not forget Edom's conduct either. Balaam, in one of his prophecies shortly afterwards, said that Edom would one day be dispossessed by Israel (Num. 24:18)—presumably as a judgement for their hostility to Moses.

While the Lord would, in his good time, deal with Edom, this did not mean that Israel could retaliate in any way they chose. They were not to follow the example of Edom, stooping to their level of grudge-holding. They could be confident that 'the Judge of all the earth [would] do what is just' (Gen. 18:25), rather than take matters into their own hands. The same applies to us, as Paul explains to the Christians in Rome: 'Beloved, never avenge yourselves, but leave it to the wrath of God, for it is written, "Vengeance is mine, I will repay, says the Lord"' (Rom. 12:19).

There was another way in which Israel could learn from Edom (as we can too). The Lord had given Edom a land ('the hill country of Seir', Gen. 36:8), and when the Lord gives a land to a people it stays given; it remains theirs. Even the food and water that the land produced belonged to them (Deut. 2:6). Not only did the Lord give Edom the land, he also drove out the Horites who lived there previously. If the Lord had enabled Esau's descendants to settle in *their* land, then surely Israel could trust him to do the same for them—that was Moses' argument (Deut. 2:12, 22). And Moses didn't forget that the Edomites were Israel's brothers (2:8), something that Israel were urged to remember too (23:7).

Joshua, nearing the end of his life, also reminded the people that God had assigned 'the hill country of Seir' (Josh. 24:4) to Esau, even as he recalled the wonderful way in which the Lord had so recently given them the promised land. While Edom were to be left alone for as long as they remained content within their own domain, it would be another story if they aligned themselves with Israel's enemies. When they did so they were 'routed' (1 Sam. 14:47) in the days of Saul, and 'subdued' (2 Sam. 8:11) by David (see Ps. 60; 108:9-10, and the questions in the 'Further Study' section at the end of this chapter). Solomon's reign saw 'Hadad the Edomite ... of the royal house in Edom' (1 Kings 11:14) being a thorn in Israel's side (11:25). Edom 'revolted from the rule of Judah' (2 Kings 8:20) while Jehoram was on the throne. Yet another quarrel is referred to in 2 Kings 14, one which Amaziah, king of Judah, got the better of (v. 10; see also 2 Chr. 25:19–20). And then there was the final clash recorded in the Bible surrounding the circumstances of Jerusalem's fall to the Babylonians. We have already seen that this was the most likely occasion for Obadiah's prophecy. It was the point at which relations between the two nations reached a new low, at the same time as Israel's fortunes hit rock bottom.

The ancient rivalry even continued into the New Testament. The three Herods we meet there were all of Edomite (by this time referred to as Idumaean) descent. The first Herod showed all the malice of his ancestors towards the Jews. The second mocked the Lord Jesus in his sufferings just as his forebears had mocked the people of God. Then the third exhibited all the pride that characterized his nation in Obadiah's day. His doom was immediate, and every bit as solemn as Edom's (Acts 12:23).

Concerning the 'vision'

The prophecy is described in the opening verse as a 'vision'. Sometimes this term is used to describe a state of consciousness in which the prophet actually sees images either of the future or of spiritually symbolic scenes, but that is not always the case. It is a term that can also be used to describe prophetic insight regarding the future without any obvious visual element (1 Sam. 3:1; 1 Chr. 17:15). While the visual element isn't obvious in Obadiah, there is certainly drama, as if the prophet is at least seeing things in his mind's eye.

Concerning the 'messenger'

Obadiah opens by telling us that he is reporting something that he first heard from the Lord: 'a messenger has been sent among the nations.' Who is the messenger? Again, we don't know. There may actually have been a particular individual doing the rounds of the neighbouring nations, gathering them together to fight Edom. If so, he was probably despatched by one of the countries nearby. What really matters is that the Lord sent him. This mysterious messenger was doing the Lord's bidding, whether he realized it or not. The Lord God was in control, even in the midst of international turmoil that appeared to be anything but under control. When Jerusalem was being ransacked, it couldn't have seemed to Israel as if God was directing events. Similarly, there will be plenty of times in our own lives when the sovereignty of God is not evident, but that doesn't mean that it is non-existent. His ways aren't our ways (Isa. 55:8), so we will often be surprised by them. They may be perplexing, but they are perfect (Ps. 18:30).

> There will be plenty of times in our own lives when the sovereignty of God is not evident, but that doesn't mean that it is non-existent.

This 'messenger' doesn't have to refer to a real person. It is possible that this is an angelic messenger ensuring that God's purposes are carried forward. It could even be a vivid poetic way of depicting the Lord's secret—but nonetheless effective—activity in providence, whereby he stirs up the surrounding countries without the use of a human instrument.

Obadiah is making it clear that, even in the wake of Jerusalem's fall, the Lord's purposes are proceeding according to plan. He is the one pulling all the strings, though in such a way that the nations are still responsible for their decisions and actions. So whatever the right understanding of this 'messenger' is, the upshot remains the same. The nations are about to 'rise against [Edom] for battle' (v. 1), and it is the Lord ('I' in v. 2) who is behind the forthcoming events. Edom thinks all is well (as we shall see), but when it is the Lord marshalling forces against you, there can be only one outcome.[2]

At the time of Obadiah's ministry it looked as if Edom had escaped the fate that Jerusalem had just suffered. To all outward appearances Israel could well be on their way out of existence, while Edom remained safe and secure. But prophets see the big picture over the long haul—and that gives a very different perspective, both on recent events and future fortunes. Edom was the nation that would ultimately disappear from the scene, while Israel would one day know an escape of its own: an escape that would last for ever.

Concerning the New Testament

Although Obadiah is not quoted in the New Testament there are two telling references to Esau. The first is in chapter 9 of Paul's letter to the Romans, where he anticipates an objection that his readers might raise against the gospel.

Given the large-scale rejection of the gospel among the Jews, some might think that God's promise and purpose had, at least in some way, failed (Rom. 9:6). Not so, says Paul. Throughout the Old Testament God had his chosen people. Yes, he had chosen Abraham, but the choosing didn't stop there. It wasn't the case that everybody descended from Abraham was among God's people. Isaac was chosen, not Ishmael, and then Jacob was chosen, not Esau. Those who weren't chosen were, in a very real sense, rejected, and that rejection had consequences. It certainly did for Esau and his descendants. Paul quotes from Malachi (the last book of our Old Testament), which was written at a time when those consequences were particularly obvious, with Edom in a low condition. The people of Israel in Malachi's day were failing to recognize God's love for them, so Malachi encouraged them to take a look at their old enemy, Edom. Surely seeing the contrast in their fortunes would help Israel see how good God had been to them, while his rejection of Edom was there for all to see. Talking in terms of 'love' and 'hatred' (Mal. 1:2–3; Rom. 9:12) might sound extreme, but it is just another way of describing God's choice of some and rejection of others—which is exactly Paul's point. If your reaction to all this is that it sounds unfair, that is just the reaction Paul expects (you can read on in Rom. 9:19–23 to see his response). So Paul uses Esau as an example of someone rejected by God. The Psalms portray the nation of Edom in a similar light.

The second reference to Esau in the New Testament comes in the letter to the Hebrews. The readers have just been encouraged to 'strive for ... holiness' (Heb. 12:14) and are then warned about two dangers. The first is the possibility that a 'root of bitterness' could spring up and cause trouble; the second is that they could follow Esau's example and so miss out on God's blessings. As with the passage in Romans, Esau's rejection by God is prominent (Heb. 12:17). Here, though, we see that this came only after *he* had rejected his birthright (12:16). Esau is portrayed as a prime example of someone who was 'sexually immoral' and 'unholy'. He had no appetite for spiritual blessing, just an appetite for stew. He was prepared to trade a wonderful inheritance for the quick satisfaction of his physical cravings. He was what we might call a 'carnal' man, and, though he lived to regret his choice, that was that.[3] So first the man and then the nation became a standing warning against making short-term choices without thinking of the long-term consequences. Esau couldn't wait—much like the prodigal son. His promised inheritance held no attraction for him while the smell of a good meal filled his nostrils. How much worse when *we* fail to look beyond the physical and temporal to the spiritual and eternal. It's one of the many lessons that Obadiah has for us.

Concerning us

Obadiah's prophecy answers two questions that the people of God would inevitably have been asking: Will Edom get away with it? ('it' being the latest and greatest in a long list of malicious episodes); and: Will we ever recover? The greater part of the book deals with the first question, giving a resounding 'No!' The close of the book answers the second question with an equally definite 'Yes!' They are both questions that we still find ourselves asking today.

The media tell us about the latest atrocity carried out on

the orders of a murderous dictator and we wonder whether he will ever be brought to justice. The message of Obadiah is designed to reassure us. Sometimes justice catches up with evil people in this life; sometimes it doesn't. But justice will be done. It may not happen until this life is over and Jesus returns, but it will be done.

We look at the state of the Christian church in our land and wonder whether anything can arrest its decline. There may be times of revival just around the corner (and surely all Christians will want to pray, in submission to God's will, for such God-glorifying times). Alternatively, such times may lie in the more distant future. It is even possible that we have had the last revival before Christ's return. But he *will* return. Then our questions will be answered once and for all. Both answers focus our thoughts on one future day that will have eternal consequences for all: 'the day of the LORD' (Obad. 15). That will be a day when justice finally catches up with many, but when salvation arrives for many others.

FOR FURTHER STUDY

1. Read Psalm 60. What is the significance of Edom in the closing verses, and what is the main point being made?

2. Read Psalm 108. While the closing verses are the same as those in Psalm 60, how is the tone of this psalm different? In what way are the repeated verses used differently in each psalm?

3. Read Psalm 83. Again we find Edom listed among Israel's enemies. What is the psalmist concerned about at the beginning? How might he draw encouragement from what he says in verses 9 to 12? On what does he base the appeal of the closing verse?

4. What other biblical examples can you think of where people made unwise short-term choices, failing to think of the long-term consequences?

TO THINK ABOUT AND DISCUSS

1. When was the last time you were concerned that someone was getting away with something? Has this happened to you on a more personal level, when someone has treated you badly without having to face any consequences?

2. Can you think of times in your own life when you felt that you would never get through a particular situation or never recover from a painful experience? Looking back, how do you think you may have benefited from them?

3. How many examples can you come up with of times when you have made poor choices based on short-term considerations? What might help us to think more long term (i.e. with an eternal perspective)?

4. What examples can you see in the world around you of an 'instant' mentality? How does Western democracy tend to promote short-term thinking in politics? In what ways are we often encouraged to gratify our immediate desires, and discouraged from thinking about consequences?

2 Deceived by pride

(vv. 2–4)

Pride is a dreadful sin. Not only does it detract from God's glory, but it also deceives the one who is proud. As we eavesdrop on the language of Edom's proud heart we get some helpful pointers as to how it deludes and ultimately destroys.

'**H**ey, listen to this …' That is the force of the 'Behold' at the beginning of verse 2. It is partly a call to pay attention, and partly an indication that what is about to be said has real shock value. Here is a message Edom is not expecting. The nation will find it hard to take the Lord's declaration seriously. It thinks of itself as chief among the nations, but it is going to be made least among the nations (v. 2). It will be made to *feel* small too.

Pride makes us big; God makes us small. The word translated 'small' in verse 2 is the same one used to describe Saul in the book of Samuel (1 Sam. 15:17). It was used of him at a time when he had a fairly accurate assessment of himself. His immediate reaction to Samuel's commendation was one of modesty. Modesty to a fault, perhaps (see 1 Sam. 10:22), but still modesty. Sadly, this perspective didn't last long. All too quickly he got too big for his boots.

Edom thought it ought to be admired, but the Lord decreed that it would be 'utterly despised' (v. 2). An earlier enemy of Israel—Sennacherib—had suffered a similar fate (Isa. 37:22). His crime had parallels with Edom's as well. The Assyrian commander had 'mocked and reviled' the people of Jerusalem, and in doing so had spoken against 'the Holy One of Israel' (2 Kings 19:21–22). The tables would soon be turned, however, and he would be despised by the people he had so recently been pouring scorn on.

The use of the word 'despised' was no accident. The father of the nation, Esau, had infamously 'despised [same Hebrew word] his birthright' (Gen. 25:34) when he sold it to his brother in return for some bread and lentil stew. Despising the Lord, or his gifts, has its consequences. How was David's terrible sin with Bathsheba summed up? 'Why have you despised the word of the LORD? ... because you have despised me [the LORD] ...' (2 Sam. 12:9–10). Israel's leaders in Ezekiel's day had 'despised [the] holy things' of the Lord (Ezek. 22:8), and in the time of Malachi the priests had similarly despised God's name (Mal. 1:6–7). The Lord told both groups that he would deal with them (Ezek. 22:14; Mal. 2:1–9). The despisers would ultimately be despised (Mal. 2:9). Psalm 73 even tells us that the arrogant and wicked will be despised by the Lord himself (Ps. 73:20). We also read of those who despise the word of the Lord (Num. 15:31; 2 Chr. 36:16), but the worst crime of all must surely be to join those who despise and reject the Saviour (Isa. 53:3). Of course, the sufferings Isaiah is describing in that chapter are what give us hope. Because we have a Saviour who was 'wounded for our transgressions' (Isa. 53:5) we can share the assurance of a sinner like David who knew that, despite his despicable sins, 'a broken and contrite heart' is something that God 'will not despise' (Ps. 51:17).

Easily deceived (v. 3)

The Lord knows what Edom's reaction will be to the announcement that they are going to be cut down to size: 'No way!' But they have been 'deceived'. That is to say, they have been convinced that something is true when in fact it isn't. The thing about being deceived is that, by definition, you don't realize it. We have a very subtle enemy who is 'the deceiver' (Rev. 12:9; see also 20:3, 8). Eve didn't realize that she had been deceived by him until it was too late. His aims haven't changed over the millennia. Paul knew that the Christians in Corinth could easily 'be led astray from a sincere and pure devotion to Christ' by the same 'cunning' adversary (2 Cor. 11:3). Twenty-first-century Christians are no different.

The devil isn't our only problem; we also have an enemy within to contend with. We are frighteningly good at deceiving ourselves. The trouble, as Jeremiah put it, is that 'the heart is deceitful above all things' (Jer. 17:9). It is particularly easy to be deceived about ourselves because arriving at an accurate, objective assessment of our abilities, strengths and weaknesses is no easy matter. Reality TV programmes are chock-a-block with people lacking a realistic appreciation of their gifts. Usually they err on the hopelessly optimistic side, though occasionally the truly talented seem unaware of just how gifted they are.

Moses warned Israel of how their hearts could be deceived, with a descent into idolatry being the result (Deut. 11:16). We are prone to tell ourselves what we want to hear, just as we are more likely to listen to those who tell us 'smooth things' (Isa. 30:10). That's what the people in Zedekiah's reign were doing. They needed to hear a less palatable truth: 'Do not deceive yourselves, saying, "The Chaldeans will surely go away from us", for they will not go away' (Jer. 37:9).

> We are prone to tell ourselves what we want to hear, just as we are more likely to listen to those who tell us 'smooth things' (Isa. 30:10).

The warnings about self-deception don't fade away in the New Testament; if anything, they intensify. Paul, James and John are all concerned about how susceptible Christians are to self-deception. The Galatian Christians thought that they could benefit from Christian teaching without bearing any responsibility towards their teachers. Wrong! 'Do not be deceived: God is not mocked, for whatever one sows, that will he also reap' (Gal. 6:7). They needed to be investing in their spiritual welfare—sowing to the Spirit, as Paul puts it (Gal. 6:8).

We easily convince ourselves that something will be all right, despite the warnings of Scripture (and sometimes conscience). The Christians at Corinth thought they could closely associate with the wicked without any problems, but Paul couldn't be clearer: 'Do not be deceived: "Bad company ruins good morals"' (1 Cor. 15:33).

It is even more serious when we convince ourselves that we are in good spiritual shape when we aren't. The Corinthians were in danger of thinking that they could inherit the kingdom of God regardless of their conduct. Paul doesn't beat about the bush: 'Do not be deceived: neither the sexually immoral, nor idolaters, nor adulterers, nor men who practise homosexuality, nor thieves, nor the greedy, nor drunkards, nor revilers, nor swindlers will inherit the kingdom of God' (1 Cor. 6:10). James has similar concerns when he addresses some who are keen hearers of God's Word but who never actually get round to putting what they learn into practice. He also warns those who think that they are very religious and yet who have no control over their tongues. He tells both groups that they are deceived (James 1:22, 26). Have you ever given any thought to the possibility that you could be deceived as to whether or not you are a genuine Christian?

Easily lifted up (vv. 3–4)

Two New Testament examples of self-deception are particularly relevant to Obadiah. Some Corinthian Christians thought that they were wise, but, sadly, they weren't thinking of the wisdom which comes from God. It was the kind of wisdom that the world values and admires: the wisdom of 'this age' (1 Cor. 3:18). In Galatia, other Christians were in danger of thinking that they were something, when in reality they were nothing (Gal. 6:3). Both churches had the same problem: pride. Pride was the culprit. Pride was doing the deceiving. It tells us lies about ourselves—nice lies. It gives us a view of ourselves, our gifts and our achievements that is not grounded in reality. It gives us a distorted view that massages our ego and puffs us up. We are left thinking that we are better than we really are—or stronger, or smarter. And before we know it, pride has deceived us.

Pharaoh didn't think he needed to listen to Moses (Exod. 5:2). Aaron and Miriam thought they could lead Israel just as well as Moses (Num. 12). King Uzziah thought he was every bit as qualified as the priests to burn incense in the temple (2 Chr. 26:16–18). Nebuchadnezzar thought that he ruled the world (Dan. 4:28–30). Simon Peter was convinced that he would never deny the Lord (Matt. 26:35). Pride had deceived them.

Sometimes we can think of pride as an outward thing—a facial expression, a tone of voice, a dismissive gesture. Here in verse 3 it is made clear that Edom's pride has its root in the heart, as does all true pride. And then we hear what kind of language a proud heart speaks. You can be sure that it will have a lot of 'I's and 'me's in it, like the words spoken by the rich farmer and by the Pharisee in the temple (Luke 12:16-19; 18:11–12). They spoke out loud; we are generally a bit more subtle. We have quite a lot of thoughts that we would never utter out loud. Often they come and go and we hardly notice them. We might be speaking wonderfully modest, humble, self-effacing words to someone else, even as our hearts are saying something very different on the inside. Hearing our inner thoughts would immediately alert us to how inappropriate they are. We need to listen more carefully to our thoughts, and monitor them more closely. Pride is so dangerous; taking steps to guard against it is vital.

The Edomites weren't worried about guarding against pride. They were revelling in it. Their pride was telling them something that was untrue. Of course, the most effective lies contain a substantial element of truth, and that was the case here. Where the Edomites lived was one factor: 'in the clefts of the rock, in [their] lofty dwelling' is how Obadiah puts it. Although the town of Petra was yet to be built, the terrain for which it is famous was already there. High up and inaccessible, Edom's territory was similarly difficult to get to and easy to defend. Their location had lulled them into a false sense of security. In many ways their confidence was understandable, but pride breeds complacency. That is why it so often goes before destruction (Prov. 16:18; 18:12). The parallel passage in Jeremiah tells us about another source of their pride. There we are told, 'The horror you inspire has deceived you' (Jer. 49:16). So as well as their position of strength, their reputation for military strength had gone to their heads.

> The most effective lies contain a substantial element of truth.

Easily brought down (v. 4)

The other disastrous error that pride makes is to leave a sovereign, almighty God out of the equation. Edom asks its 'Who will bring me down?' question in verse 3, assuming the reply, 'There is no one capable of bringing you down to the ground.' Instead comes the Lord's answer: 'I will' (v. 4).

Nothing is too hard for him (Gen. 18:14). They could have been even harder to get to, even higher up, but it would have made no difference. Bringing down 'the mighty from their thrones' (Luke 1:52) is God's speciality.

For further study ▶

FOR FURTHER STUDY

1. Read 1 Samuel 13:8–14; 15:9–31. What signs of pride can you see in Saul's behaviour and words in these passages?

2. Read Malachi 1:6–14. How exactly had the people despised the Lord's name? Why didn't they realize that was what they were doing? Can you think of twenty-first-century ways of despising the name of the Lord without realizing it?

3. Read Luke 12:16–19; 18:11–12. How is the language of these two men similar, and what does it tell us about pride? In what ways were these men deceived?

TO THINK ABOUT AND DISCUSS

1. How many ways can you think of that the devil uses to deceive us? What is he most interested in deceiving us about?

2. How many things can you think of that we can get proud about?

3. Can you provide examples of what we say in our hearts when we are under the influence of pride?

4. What sorts of lies do we most want to believe?

3 Deceived by allies

(vv. 5–7)

These verses tell us that Edom is in for a double surprise. Both the thoroughness with which it is to be pillaged and the betrayal that leads to it will catch the people unawares. They just don't see it coming—but Obadiah does!

We already know that Edom is to be brought down. Now we find out what that will involve.

The extent of the destruction (vv. 5–6)

First, the extent of the judgement is dramatically underlined. We are given two illustrations of what will *not* be happening to Edom.

Burglars are selective: electrical goods, jewellery, car keys. They usually know what they are looking for, so that they can be gone before they are spotted or any alarm is raised. There is a limit to what they want and what they can take. Their aim is to get what they can sell on for their own profit, not to destroy the home of their victim. But this kind of cherry-picking thievery is not what lies in store for Edom. Their fate will be far worse.

Then there were the laws surrounding grape-gathering. The poor were to be catered for (literally!). Workers had to be careful not to strip the vineyards or gather the fallen grapes (Lev. 19:9–10). There were to be generous leftovers for those reduced to begging. The people of Israel were to reflect their God's care for the poor and homeless. The book of Ruth tells of how she benefited from this practice in the fields at the time of the barley harvest. Edom's enemies, on the other hand, would not spare a thought for the poor and hungry when they began to asset-strip the land. The kind of plundering which Edom was to face would be of a different order altogether. Their plunderers, unlike the God of Israel, would show no mercy. Edom would be 'stripped … bare', as Jeremiah puts it (Jer. 49:10).

There would be no place to hide—either for the Edomites or for their valuables. They needn't think that they would get enough prior warning to find safe hidey-holes for themselves. Nor would they be able to stash belongings and then return to reclaim them at a later date. Their treasures would be 'sought out' (v. 6).

We get very attached to our 'treasures'. It's not only pride that deceives—so do riches (Matt. 13:22; Mark 4:19). They convince us that they are what life is all about (Luke 12:15). They take our thoughts away from the word of God (Matt. 13:22) and seduce our hearts. Before we know it, we are following the unhappy example of the foolish farmer who '[laid] up treasure for himself' and was not 'rich towards God' (Luke 12:21). Our Saviour has warned us, 'Do not lay up for yourselves treasures on earth … For where your treasure is, there your heart will be also' (Matt. 6:19, 21). If we are not very careful, having captured our hearts, 'the love of money' will lead us into 'all kinds of evil' (1 Tim. 6:10). 'You cannot serve God and money' (Matt. 6:24).

As Jonah found out, you can't hide from God (Jonah 1:3–4). The book of Revelation (quoting from Isaiah) tells us that there will be many on the day of judgement who will make the same discovery. They will be 'calling to the mountains and rocks, "Fall on us and hide us from the face of him who is seated on the throne, and from the wrath of the Lamb"' (Rev. 6:16).

Achan learned that, not only is it impossible to hide from God, but you can't hide *things* from him either (Josh. 7:1, 20–23). The beautiful cloak, silver shekels and gold bar were just as visible to God when they were buried under the tent as they were when they were 'laid … down before the LORD' (7:23). God knows the heart of every individual and the balance of every secret bank account. He knows what we have got and what we are doing with it. And what he has entrusted to us he is well able to withdraw in an instant, as the Edomites would discover. The judgement they could expect would involve their enemies taking everything and leaving nothing. They would be picked clean, with no cause for complaint: 'with the measure you use it will be measured to you' (Matt. 7:2).

Their judgement would be detailed and thorough, and so will ours. Jesus said so: 'on the day of judgement people will give account for every careless word they speak' (Matt. 12:36). 'Nothing is covered up that will not be revealed, or hidden that will not be known' (Luke 12:2). Paul even warns those in Christian service that the quality of their work will be tested too: 'Now if anyone builds on the foundation [Jesus Christ] with gold, silver, precious stones, wood, hay, straw— each one's work will become manifest, for the Day will disclose it, because it will be revealed by fire, and the fire will test what sort of work each one has done' (1 Cor. 3:12–13). It is possible to do things in our lives that are impressive and widely admired, but which will not stand up to the scrutiny of the last day.

Then it won't be possible to put a positive spin on things, to exaggerate, misrepresent or in any other way give a false impression. All will be 'stripped … bare' (Jer. 49:10)—a terrifying prospect for unbelievers, and a sobering one for Christians. There won't be any condemnation on that day for Christians, but there will be a few surprises when rewards are distributed according to what was really going on behind the scenes and in people's hearts. One thing we can be sure of: 'many who are first will be last, and the last first' (Matt. 19:30).

The source of the destruction (v. 7)

Who will be responsible for Esau's destruction? Supposed allies. The Edomites will find themselves fleeing from those they thought were their friends. Instead of helping to keep other nations at bay, they will be driving the people of Edom out of their homeland. Instead of being dependable, their friends will prove deceitful. It will be a bitter pill to swallow, a betrayal of the worst kind.

When a brother in arms takes up arms against you, it hurts. When someone who has eaten at your table plots against you in league with those more interested in devouring *you*, it cuts deep. It has to rank high in any table of adverse experiences. That's what happens when we rely on alliances and treaties with fellow sinners. The sad truth is that they can't be trusted, and neither can we.

It's not just the devil and our own hearts that can deceive us. The apostle John warns us that there are many doing the devil's work for him (1 John 2:26; 3:7). Whether it is Jacob deceiving Isaac, Laban deceiving Jacob or the Gibeonites deceiving Joshua, the lesson is the same: we need to be aware of the possibility that we might be deceived by others. Even those who speak in God's name aren't to be taken on trust. Prophets in Jeremiah's day were preaching 'the deceit of their own minds' (Jer. 14:14). It was a nice, reassuring message, but it wasn't from the Lord, and it wasn't true. The New Testament has a special cautionary word for us about deceptive false teachers (Rom. 16:18; Eph. 5:6; 2 Thes. 2:3). We need to be as wise as serpents and as innocent as doves in our dealings with others.

It is a sad fact that we are all too quick to trust those undeserving of our confidence, while at the same time being woefully slow to trust in the One infinitely worthy of our trust. Suffering from a blockade imposed by King Baasha of Israel,

> We are all too quick to trust those undeserving of our confidence, while at the same time being woefully slow to trust in the One infinitely worthy of our trust.

Asa, king of Judah, turned to the king of Syria for help. But for Syria to enter into a covenant with Judah would mean Syria breaking their covenant with Israel. Such are the covenants of men: entered into and broken according to convenience. Not so with the everlasting covenant of a faithful God. And yet it was this God Asa wouldn't rely on. No wonder Hanani was sent to confront Asa about such a foolish course of action. Fancy preferring to rely on the king of Syria rather than on the Lord his God—especially given that the Lord had proved himself faithful in a similar situation in the past (2 Chr. 16:1–8)! Asa's successor, Jehoshaphat, also got himself into trouble through an ill-advised alliance, with Ahaz and even Hezekiah following suit.

Throughout Old Testament history, nations were never slow to join forces against the people of God. The New Testament tells us about one of the more unlikely alliances—this time against the Son of God—when we read of how 'Herod and Pilate became friends with each other' (Luke 23:12). Not far into the book of Acts we see others ganging up on Jesus' followers (Acts 4:24–30), a practice that has continued to the present day. We will have to face alliances against the Christian church. The only alliance that makes sense for us, the only alliance that can safely be trusted, is one with a faithful God, founded on a reliable covenant.

The remarkable thing is that this God is prepared to enter into a covenant with those who have proved themselves to be covenant-breakers over and over again. Although theologians have, at times, made more of it than the Bible does, the rules of the garden of Eden amount to something very much like a covenant, and, ever since, Adam's descendants have been following his example. No sooner had Moses delivered the Ten Commandments and confirmed the covenant with the people than they were breaking it. From then on, Israel's history could be described as a serial breaking and renewing of the covenant. Christians are made of the same stuff. Thankfully, the new covenant makes fuller and clearer provision for our unfaithfulness than did the old. Every time we take part in the Lord's Supper we have reason to acknowledge that we have failed in our covenant commitments, even as we celebrate our Saviour's successful sealing of the covenant with his blood. Despite all of our betrayals, Jesus' love for us led him willingly to suffer the pain of betrayal. This was no small part of his sufferings. David experienced real heartache when betrayed by his counsellor Ahithophel and his son Absalom. We know that because he put his feelings into words in two psalms (Ps. 41:9; 55:13–14, 20). And the Lord quoted David as Judas' betrayal drew near (John 13:18). In some ways David had only himself to blame for the betrayals he suffered. Poor parenting was certainly a factor with Absalom, and the rebellion was part of the Lord's punishment for David's sin with Bathsheba (2 Sam. 12:11). In contrast, Jesus had done nothing to deserve the treachery of Judas. We were to blame. It was for our sakes that he 'endured from sinners such hostility against himself' (Heb. 12:3). The Edomites never saw their allies' betrayal coming, whereas Jesus did. It added to his sufferings (John 13:21). Knowing exactly what awaited him in Jerusalem took its toll. Thankfully, it was a price he was prepared to pay.

For further study ▶

FOR FURTHER STUDY

1. Find passages in the New Testament that speak of rewards on the day of judgement. How do you think it will work? Establish what we know from Scripture, and then see what you think you can deduce from what is clear. Given that Christians will be freed from sin, what do you think our reaction will be to losing rewards because of our own failings?

2. Read 1 Corinthians 3:10–15. What do you think Paul had in mind when he referred to wood, hay and straw, and when he spoke of gold and silver? (A look at the wider context may help.)

3. Read Genesis 27:5–25; 29:21–27; Joshua 9:3–15. What do these examples of deception have in common, and how do they differ?

4. Read Luke 12:16–21. In what different ways was the farmer deceived?

5. How many distinct different covenants can you find in the Old Testament that are made by God?

TO THINK ABOUT AND DISCUSS

1. How do you think you will feel on the day of judgement as a Christian? Will there be elements of disappointment for the Christian? How might our having been freed from sin, and particularly pride, help?

2. How do we lay up treasure for ourselves in heaven?

3. What kinds of evil does the love of money most often lead to?

4. What sorts of things could spoil our work/achievements that would come to light only on the day of judgement?

5. In today's world, how do politicians and advertisers try to deceive us? What are the most common ways in which con men deceive their victims?

4 Deceived by complacency

(vv. 8–9)

Edom was well known for its 'wise men' and its 'mighty men'. But these verses warn that any complacency will prove to be a mistake. Their two great strengths will not shield them from the deserved judgement that is coming their way.

The Lord is going to bring Edom down. That's final. Edom may not think so, but it is. Back in verse 3 Edom had asked a rhetorical question, and now the Lord is doing the same: 'Will I not?' The Lord is asking what will stop him from dealing with Edom. The correct answer is 'Nothing!', but Edom might well have come up with two possibilities. Maybe they could scheme their way out of trouble, or, failing that, fight their way out. But they would rely on their traditional strengths in vain. Averting the coming judgement was out of the question. Even postponing it was not an option. The day had already been set.

Terrible judgement (v. 8)

When the Lord refers to 'that day' our initial reaction might well be to ask, 'Which day?' Unlike us, however, Obadiah's first hearers would have known immediately what was being referred to. The answer is, 'the day of the LORD'. That was the phrase used by many Old Testament prophets to refer to the time when the Lord judged particular nations in particular ways. Each of those 'days' also pointed forward to a definitive 'day of the LORD' when the whole world will be judged. There are times in history when the Lord deals with specific nations and specific individuals, but the end of history will see the arrival of 'the great and awesome day of the LORD' (Joel 2:31; see also 2:11) when all will be judged. So the Lord has an appointment with the nation of Edom. They (like everyone else) are going to face his judgement whether they like it or not, and whether they believe it or not.

Obadiah's prophecy will go on to talk about another day in the recent past: verses 10 to 14 talk about a day of calamity for Jerusalem (v. 13). But the day mentioned here is when Edom will be the one facing the calamity. This 'day of the LORD' (v. 15) is approaching fast.

Proverbial wisdom (vv. 8–9)

Verse 7 ended by pointing out that Edom would fail to recognize the traitorous plans of their allies. That must have been particularly galling for a nation with a reputation for shrewdness and wisdom. Job's counsellors represent the best of the world's wisdom, and one of them, Eliphaz, was a Temanite (Job 2:11). Teman was the name of one of Edom's

major towns (named after one of Esau's grandsons—Gen.
36:9–14; 1 Chr. 1:35–36), and the name was sometimes used
to mean the whole of the land (Obad. 9). Another poetic
name for Edom was Mount Esau (vv. 8–9), much as Mount
Zion is sometimes used, especially in the Psalms, as a name
for Jerusalem, or sometimes for Judah and even Israel. Its
use here serves to highlight the enmity between Edom and
Israel, depicting them as two competing mountains, as well
as underlining their very different fates.

The wisdom of Edom's counsellors, then, had become
proverbial. Today, we might speak of Oxbridge dons or
Ivy League professors. One of the last descendants of Esau
that we read about in the New Testament, King Herod,
was described by the Lord Jesus himself as 'that fox' (Luke
13:32).[1]

That the Edomites were unaware of their allies' traitorous
schemes was not purely the fault of their wise men. This was
the Lord's doing. He could have done it in two ways. If verse
8 is to be taken literally, the Lord ensured that there were
no wise men around in Edom just when they were needed
most. On the other hand, a not-so-literal interpretation
would be (along the lines of the final clause) that he simply
withheld understanding from those who usually provided
wise counsel. Either way, any confidence that Edom placed in
the astuteness of their chief advisers was going to meet with
disappointment.

The Lord has various ways of working out his purposes.
Having been betrayed by his valued adviser, Ahithophel,
David prayed, 'O LORD, please turn the counsel of Ahithophel
into foolishness' (2 Sam. 15:31). Interestingly, the Lord came

to David's aid in a different way from the one envisaged by David. Rather than turning Ahithophel's counsel into foolishness, the Lord ensured that Absalom ignored Ahithophel's characteristically wise counsel (2 Sam. 17:14).

The Lord has made us with minds, and we are supposed to use them. Common sense is a gift from God that we should use to the full. But we mustn't trust in it. Sometimes God's way defies all common sense and received wisdom. That is why we should always approach decisions prayerfully, however clear the right choice might appear to us. Acting on our own assessment of the situation without prayer is unwise, however perceptive and usually accurate we are. In the Bible's account of David's life it is noticeable that the periods in his life when all was well in his relationship with the Lord were marked by times when he 'enquired of the Lord' (1 Sam. 23:2, 4; 30:8; 2 Sam. 2:1; 5:19, 23). The Lord's thoughts aren't our thoughts and his ways aren't our ways, as Isaiah reminds us (Isa. 55:8–9). That is why we can't afford to 'lean on [our] own understanding', but need 'in all [our] ways' to 'acknowledge him' (Prov. 3:5–6). Use your understanding, certainly, but don't lean on it!

> Sometimes God's way defies all common sense and received wisdom.

It's so easy to think we're smart enough to work things out for ourselves. Our academic background may persuade us, or we may pride ourselves on being graduates of 'the university of life', but one way or another most of us are easily convinced that we know best—even on the flimsiest of evidence and the minimum of background knowledge.

Without any political experience we think we could run the country. With no sporting gifts of our own we think we could lead our favourite football team to success. The growth of talk shows in the media has only encouraged us to think that our opinions, no matter how ignorant and uninformed, are as valid as the next person's.

In churches, too, many Christians seem to think they could do a better job than their elders. Perhaps the most shocking instance of an 'I know best' attitude is that of Simon Peter. The Lord had been speaking of the sufferings that awaited him in Jerusalem, only for Simon Peter to contradict him and insist that the cross was something to avoid rather than to embrace. He thought he knew best when, in reality, his was the worst possible of plans. Jesus even made it clear that the idea of avoiding the cross was not simply unwise but of the devil (Matt. 16:23; Mark 8:33).

A healthy Christian outlook includes a profound awareness of our ignorance and folly. The right response is, as James advises us, to turn to the only wise God (Rom. 16:27) and ask him for wisdom (James 1:5). Nebuchadnezzar needed wisdom to explain his troubling dream. He had a whole host of people to call on for assistance but only Daniel was able to help. We are left in no doubt where Daniel's help came from: 'Blessed be the name of God for ever and ever … he gives wisdom to the wise and knowledge to those who have understanding' (Dan. 2:20–21).

Formidable strength (v. 9)

If wisdom is one area where pride can deceive us and make us self-confident, self-reliant and complacent, strength is another. Wisdom and might are often referred to together in Scripture. After interpreting Nebuchadnezzar's dream, Daniel said to him that it was his God 'to whom belong wisdom and might' (Dan. 2:20), and he went on to give thanks to God, saying, 'you have given me wisdom and might' (2:23). In the New Testament Paul warned the Corinthians against 'the wisdom of the world' (1 Cor. 1:20), telling them that Christ is 'the wisdom of God' but also 'the power of God' (1 Cor. 1:24).

We are frighteningly quick to trust in our own strength, even when there is all too much evidence of how weak we really are. Perceived and reputed military strength was what made Edom complacent. They would have agreed with what Napoleon is supposed to have said: 'God fights on the side with the best artillery.'[2] The Old Testament has its fair share of over-confident generals. More than one commander-in-chief could have benefited from King Ahab's warning: 'Let not him who straps on his armour boast himself as he who takes it off' (1 Kings 20:11). At a more personal level, Samson displayed the same misplaced trust in his own strength when he said to himself, 'I will go out as at other times and shake myself free' (Judg. 16:20). He had forgotten the Lord, and failed to realize that 'the LORD had left him'. Simon Peter also over-estimated the strength of his courage when he claimed, 'Even if I must die with you, I will not deny you!' (Matt. 26:35). Sadly, we are no less inclined to over-confidence when it comes to ourselves and our spiritual warfare. Strangely, what we really need if we are to be ready for spiritual battle is a sense of our weakness. Feeling strong is dangerous. We might be comparatively strong in human terms, but we are no match for the devil. That is why we cannot afford to be independent, tackling challenges in our own strength. Feeling weak, on the other hand, should encourage us to rely on the God who is 'the strength of his people' (Ps. 28:8). That's what Paul found. He was troubled by what he called 'a thorn … in the flesh' (2 Cor. 12:7). We don't know what that was exactly—probably some kind of ailment—but we do know that it made Paul feel weak. After he prayed three times that the Lord would rid him of the problem, the answer came back: 'My grace is sufficient for you, for my power is made perfect in weakness' (2 Cor. 12:9). So weakness is no bad thing. The only way to be truly strong is to be strengthened by God.

David had his 'mighty men' (2 Sam. 23:8–39), and so did Edom. With its impregnable location and wise counsellors, an elite fighting force appeared to be the final piece of the jigsaw. We could almost say of Edom, 'If anyone else thinks he has reason for confidence in the flesh, [they had] more' (Phil. 3:4). But an 'arm of flesh' is no match for 'the LORD our God' (2 Chr. 32:8). Mighty they may have been, but Edom's elite soldiers would not triumph. Instead, according to the Lord's promise (Exod. 23:27), they would be 'dismayed' (or 'thrown into confusion', 'thrown into a panic', Exod. 23:27; Josh. 10:10—the Hebrew word is the same). 'Dismayed' is really an understatement. 'Slaughter' was what faced them, and it would extend to 'every man'. To be 'cut off' was the punishment that would fit the crime (v. 14).

For further study ▶

1. Read Isaiah 13:6–13 and Amos 5:18–20. What else do these passages tell us about 'the day of the LORD', and what potential misunderstandings about that day do they guard against? What suggests that these descriptions are of more than just a (relatively) small judgement on a particular nation?

2. Read 2 Corinthians 12:1–10. How does the connection between pride and strength here parallel Edom's situation, and how does it differ?

3. Consult commentaries (and/or the Internet) to see how many different possible explanations for Paul's 'thorn in the flesh' you can find. Regardless of what it actually was, what sorts of things can play the same humbling role in our lives?

4. Read 2 Chronicles 10:1–15. What factors do you think contributed to Rehoboam's decision to follow the young men's advice?

TO THINK ABOUT AND DISCUSS

1. When was the last time you thought you knew best, only to be proved wrong?

2. What do you consider to be your strengths? How could this lead to complacency?

3. What experiences in your life have left you feeling particularly weak? Did they have a beneficial effect on your spiritual health?

4. Can you think of any famous examples in history where complacency led to disaster?

5 The day of your brother

(vv. 10–14)

In these verses we learn where the people of Edom had gone wrong. They had treated 'their brother Jacob' as if they were hostile foreigners. At first they had been mere spectators, but by the end they were active aggressors—something the Lord would not overlook.

The punishment (v. 10)

The words 'violence' and 'brother' are designed to jar against each other. Edom had brought together two words that should have remained apart. Using the name 'Jacob' is a reminder that this was no distant relation, not even a half-brother, but a twin brother. Instead of brotherly love there had been malice and hostility. It was shameful, so proud Edom would be shamed. There is irony and emphasis in the phrase 'shame shall cover you'. The fig leaves Adam and Eve sewed together in the garden of Eden were designed to *cover* their shame. To be covered *with* shame is about the strongest way Obadiah could have put it.

We've already encountered the phrase 'cut off' (see v. 9), but just in case we haven't grasped the finality of the coming judgement, the words 'for ever' are added here. There will be no lasting recovery from the blow that is about to fall. It's a message that Malachi reinforces (Mal. 1:3–4) and that history confirms.[1]

The initial crime (v. 11)

How did it ever come to this? Where did the violence come from? Well, it all started when Edom did nothing. It's all about what they failed to do. They simply 'stood aloof'. As Edmund Burke is supposed to have said, 'All that is necessary for the triumph of evil is that good men do nothing.'[2] Most people think of sin as something that we commit, but the Bible is quite clear that it also describes things that we *omit*. As the 1662 Book of Common Prayer encourages us to confess: 'We have left undone those things which we ought to have done', as well as having done 'those things which we ought not to have done'. James's definition of sin makes the same point: 'whoever knows the right thing to do and fails to do it, for him it is sin' (James 4:17). Archbishop Ussher's[3] last words are supposed to have been, 'Lord, forgive me all my sins, and specially my sins of omission.'[4] The Lord Jesus makes

> Most people think of sin as something that we commit, but the Bible is quite clear that it also describes things that we *omit*.

it clear that, on the day of judgement, he will be concerned with what we haven't done every bit as much as with what we have done (Matt. 25:41–42). In the original Hebrew, 'stood aloof' is literally 'stood on the other side', which points us to the parable of the good Samaritan. The priest and the Levite both 'passed by on the other side', failing to be a neighbour to the injured man. Their failure was Edom's. The nation most closely related to God's people, who we might have thought would be most likely to help them in their hour of need, singularly failed to come to their assistance.

It's easy to be critical, but standing up for those who are being treated badly isn't always easy. If someone is being bullied in the classroom or workplace, it's so much easier to 'stand aloof' than to step in. And then the time comes when everybody else notices that you're not joining in and the pressure builds to at least tacitly approve. Saul may not have thrown stones at Stephen but he was looking after the coats of those who were. He was 'standing by', and that amounted to 'approving' of those who killed Stephen (Acts 22:20).

A couple of psychologists once ran a study comparing the reactions of two groups of students. The first group were about to give a talk on 'the good Samaritan', while the second were going to attend a meeting outlining possible future roles for seminary graduates. On the way to their respective gatherings all the students passed a man slumped in a corridor. The study found that the likelihood of students stopping to help the man was not significantly different between the two groups. The psychologists' report of their experiment even says, 'On several occasions, a seminary student going to give his talk on the parable of the Good Samaritan literally stepped over the victim as he hurried on his way!'[5] It's easy to smile at the irony of it all, but not so easy to know whether we would have fared any better in the same situation ...

A more sobering example of 'standing aloof' comes from the following eyewitness account dating back to the Second World War:

I lived in Germany during the Nazi Holocaust. I considered myself a Christian. We heard stories of what was happening to the Jews, but we tried to distance ourselves from it, because what could anyone do to stop it? A railroad track ran behind our small church and each Sunday morning we could hear the whistle in the distance and then the wheels coming over the tracks.

We became disturbed when we heard the cries coming from the train as it passed by. We realized that it was carrying Jews like cattle in the cars! Week after week the whistle would blow. We dreaded to hear the sound of those wheels because we knew that we could hear the cries of the Jews en route to a death camp. Their screams tormented us.

We knew the time the train was coming and when we heard the whistle blow we began singing hymns. By the time the train came past our church we were singing at the top of our voices. If we heard the screams, we sang more loudly and soon we heard them no more. Years have passed and no one talks about it anymore. But I still hear that train whistle in my sleep. God forgive me; forgive all of us who called ourselves Christians yet did nothing to intervene.[6]

There have been all too many examples in church history of times when Christians have turned a blind eye and just 'sung more loudly'—or even worse. Whether it was segregation in the USA or apartheid in South Africa the Christian church has got it wrong again and again. Sins of omission can be every bit as serious as sins of commission.

What was going on as Edom stood back added to their sin and shaped their judgement. We've already been told that Edom's treasures were going to be 'sought out' (v. 6). It was only fitting that they should eventually share Jerusalem's fate. The callousness of Judah's enemies is illustrated by their casting of lots: a scene and attitude that would be repeated by Roman soldiers at the foot of the cross (Ps. 22:18; Matt. 27:35; John 19:24).

Edom's crime is summed up at the end of verse 11: 'you were like one of them.' They should have been different. They should have swum against the current.

We should be different too. We're supposed to be salt and light in a decaying, dark world (Matt. 5:13–16). We're supposed to be without blemish in the midst of a crooked and twisted generation (Phil. 2:15). We're supposed to be in the world but not 'of' it (John 17:16). We're not supposed to 'be conformed to this world' but rather 'transformed' (Rom. 12:2). When Paul wrote to the Christians at Corinth he reeled off a kind of top-ten list of sins of their contemporaries, and then said, 'And such were some of you. But you were washed, you were sanctified, you were justified in the name of the Lord Jesus Christ and by the Spirit of God' (1 Cor. 6:11). He could have said, with Obadiah, 'you were like one of them' (v. 11), but Paul could put his stress on the 'were'. For the Corinthians, that was all in the past. Sadly, Edom had remained 'like one of them'.

Edom shouldn't have been like the strangers and

foreigners who sacked Jerusalem. They were supposed to be like brothers—loving brothers, not squabbling brothers. Blood really should be thicker than water. Family matters. 'If anyone does not provide for his relatives, and especially for members of his household, he has denied the faith and is worse than an unbeliever' (1 Tim. 5:8).

But the Christian has spiritual family too. It is important that we treat our Christian brothers and sisters with a love that reflects that special relationship. It wasn't just Paul who was grieved when he heard that in Corinth 'brother [was going] to law against brother, and that before unbelievers' (1 Cor. 6:6); love between his disciples matters to Jesus too (John 15:12–17). Sometimes Christians treat one another in a way that even the world can see is shameful. 'My brothers, these things ought not to be so' (James 3:10).

> Sins of omission are bad enough in themselves, but the reality is that they stand at the top of a very slippery slope.

The slippery slope (vv. 12–14)

Sins of omission are bad enough in themselves, but the reality is that they stand at the top of a very slippery slope. Verses 12 to 14 chart the downward course that is so easy to take.

Although the Hebrew is a series of 'Do not!' commands, it is clear from the whole context that this is not a series of warnings for the future. Edom's doom is already certain. Obadiah isn't warning them in the hope that they will listen; these verses are phrased as if the prophet is a spectator as Edom gets involved in the fall of Jerusalem. Past events are presented dramatically as if they are happening right in front of Obadiah. As he watches he shouts, 'Don't!' in horror. It is a poetic and vivid description of what has already taken place. The real force of Obadiah's words is: 'You shouldn't have ...!'

Schadenfreude (v. 12)

At the top of the slope the Edomites simply 'stood aloof'. Verse 12 tells us that Edom began its descent of the slippery slope by a change in attitude. They still weren't actually *doing* anything. It was just an attitude, still without actions, at this stage. They were gloating, rejoicing and boasting, and they shouldn't have been. Their demeanour betrayed a hostile attitude that took real pleasure in Jerusalem's 'misfortune', 'ruin' and 'distress' (v. 12).

It's a sad fact that we are such sinners that we can derive satisfaction from the suffering of others. Malice wishes others ill, and gloating is what happens when those wishes are realized. Boasting about it is a way of rubbing salt into the wound, making the sufferers aware that we are taking delight in their misery. It ought to shock us that we are all capable of such nastiness, but the Bible warns us that this is what we are like. The regularity with which we experience such unworthy feelings might also blind us to just how rotten they are.

Where do these feelings come from? Enmity. Sin makes us selfish, and selfishness introduces jealousy, rivalry, anger and conflict. If it wasn't for sin we wouldn't make or have any enemies. But sin means that anyone who crosses us, who thwarts our plans, gets in our way or stops us from doing or getting what we want becomes our 'foe'. And foes 'gloat', as

Lamentations reminds us (Lam. 1:7). That's why sports fans tend to be gloating experts. Whether it is the open hostility of football fans baiting one another with chants about past defeats, or the usually respectable golf fans unable to stifle the beginnings of a cheer when the other country's player hits the ball into the water: if you're rooting for one team you are likely to wish ill on the other. To my shame, not too long ago I caught myself deriving secret satisfaction from noticing that somebody who had recently lost a lot of weight (thus awakening jealousy in me) had put it back on again with more besides. Initially, the person had made me feel inferior, only for me then to feel superior. The German language has a word for it: *Schadenfreude*, meaning 'delight in the pain of others'. Interestingly, brain-scanning studies have shown that *Schadenfreude* is closely related to envy, and researchers have also found that people with low self-esteem are more likely to feel it. The philosopher Schopenhauer (who was no friend of Christianity) described *Schadenfreude* as 'the worst trait in human nature. It is a feeling which is closely akin to cruelty, and differs from it, to say the truth, only as theory from practice.'[7] He is also supposed to have commented, 'To feel envy is human, to savour *Schadenfreude* is devilish.'[8] If you monitor your thoughts carefully enough you probably won't have too long to wait before catching yourself at it. We all have this sin in our hearts, because we love ourselves more than our neighbours. The media cater for our appetite for seeing overpaid, over-confident politicians, celebrities or sports stars attacked or exposed in one way or another. The media also take an Edom-like delight in strife within churches and the moral failure of all too many ministers. Alas, even within Christian churches there are those who have a taste for gossip, preferring to spread rumours of bad behaviour rather than offering loving support for a stumbling brother or sister. Instead of helping them, there are even times when they'll kick them while they're down. But 'he who is glad at calamity will not go unpunished' (Prov. 17:5).

Boasting (v. 12)

The next level down the slippery slope involves our words. A hostile attitude eventually finds expression in verbal attacks. Edom boasts, or, as the Hebrew (and ESV marginal note) reads literally, 'enlarges its mouth' in response to the ruin of Jerusalem. Expressions of glee and mockery literally added insult to injury. Psalm 137 actually tells us one of the things the Edomites were saying. They were egging on the Babylonians as they reduced the city of Jerusalem to rubble, crying, 'Lay it bare, lay it bare, down to its foundations!' (Ps. 137:7). The people of God have always been on the receiving end of mockery and barbed comments. Through the Old Testament and into the New it was their lot at various points, and the centuries since have seen the same pattern repeated. Right now, around the globe, there are many Christians facing different levels of mockery and scorn.

It's not just that one sin leads to another, but also small sins so easily, and imperceptibly, lead to bigger ones. We gain speed as we descend the slippery slope. It is like the proverbial frog in water that is gradually heated up. If the temperature rises slowly enough it is said that the frog will fail to notice— even to the point that it will remain in the water until it is boiled alive.[9] Having just gone along with the bullying for a while, before you know it you are making unkind remarks, just to show the bullies that you're on their side. Then you find that you're beginning to mean what you say. And after words come actions.

Profiting and persecuting (vv. 13–14)

The next stage in Edom's downward course is that they act. But not aggressively: they simply follow Judah's enemies through the gate into Jerusalem and join in with the looting of the city. There are always more looters than rioters when there is civil unrest. The opportunity for financial gain is too much for many to resist. They may have little sympathy for the demonstration that started it all, and have no desire for violence, but they aren't averse to capitalizing on the situation.

The final verse tells us that at the bottom of the slippery slope lies active, aggressive involvement. Edom 'cut off' [10] those who fled Jerusalem and handed survivors over to their enemies. Spectators had become persecutors. Edom shouldn't have stood to one side; they shouldn't have mocked; they shouldn't have lined their own pockets at Jerusalem's expense; but most of all they shouldn't have joined in with the persecution of the city's inhabitants. Why not? Because they were persecuting the Lord's people— not a good move. The Lord certainly doesn't 'stand aloof' while his people suffer. He assures them, 'he who touches you touches the apple of his eye' (Zech. 2:8). The Lord Jesus takes it personally. That is why he asked Saul, on the road to Damascus, 'Saul, Saul, why are you persecuting *me*?' (Acts 9:4, my emphasis).

The Saviour knows and the Saviour cares

Our comfort is that we will encounter nothing that our Saviour hasn't faced before us (see Ps. 22:16–18; Heb. 12:3; and the Gospel accounts of the crucifixion). We have a high priest 'who in every respect has been tempted as we are, yet without sin' (Heb. 4:15). That includes mockery. He sympathizes with us, and he also teaches us how to meet mockery with prayer and faith (see Ps. 22:19–31). It also includes persecution. Our Saviour knows what we suffer for him (see Rev. 2–3). He'll be with us to help us at the time (Luke 21:12–15), and he assures us that our reward in heaven will be great (Matt. 5:10–11).

For further study ▶

1. Read Psalm 1. Do you see a kind of slippery slope in the opening verses? How would you describe the progression down it?

2. Read about Goliath, Sennacherib, Sanballat and Tobiah (1 Sam. 17:10, 42–44; 2 Kings 18:19–25; Neh. 4:1–3. See also Acts 2:13; 17:32). What are God's people mocked for in these passages? Are there different reasons lying behind the mockery in these examples?

3. Read Matthew 25:31–46 and Romans 2. How can we be justified by faith alone, and yet be judged according to our deeds?

4. Read Psalm 22. What do we learn about our Saviour's sufferings here that we wouldn't know otherwise? Do you think that this psalm is purely prophetic, or did David have an experience of his own that in some ways foreshadowed the Lord's?

TO THINK ABOUT AND DISCUSS

1. What do you think are the most common sins of omission?

2. What things is the Christian church in danger of turning a blind eye to today?

3. When were you last secretly pleased by someone else's difficulties? What was the main reason?

4. Who is currently being mocked in the media? What sorts of people are sufficiently unpopular to produce *Schadenfreude* in others?

5. What kinds of mockery are aimed at Christians today, and what do they tend to focus on? Can you see any examples of where mockery is beginning to head towards active persecution?

6. Find out which are the top five countries today when it comes to the persecution of Christians. How should we pray for them, and how might those persecuted Christians pray for us?

6 The day of the Lord for the nations

(vv. 15–16)

Obadiah's vision now begins to see things through a wide-angled lens. Up until now we have been focused on Edom, but they will not be alone in facing God's judgement. 'All the nations' are answerable to the 'Lord of all the earth' (Josh. 3:11, 13; Ps. 97:5; Zech. 6:5). Their judgement will be final, with no prospect of recovery.

A day of reckoning (v. 15)

Why should Edom have behaved differently? Because 'the day of the LORD is near'. The nearness of judgement ought to have changed the way the people conducted themselves. Instead, they acted as if there was no final reckoning to face; as if they could do what they liked. 'Because the sentence against an evil deed is not executed speedily, the heart of the children of man is fully set to do evil'

(Eccles. 8:11). The right use of a gracious delay is to repent, as Paul and Peter explain (Rom. 2:4; 2 Peter 3:9). The way we live each day should be profoundly affected by the approach of 'the day of the LORD'. Paul kept the prospect of that day in mind as he ministered, and it seems to have dominated his thoughts increasingly as his ministry drew to a close (2 Cor. 4:16–5:11; 2 Tim. 1:12, 18; 4:1, 8, 18). John makes it plain that it should have a similar influence on all who share the same hope (1 John 3:2–3).

There's a scene in the 1989 film *Casualties of War* in which an American soldier in Vietnam, Private Eriksson (played by Michael J. Fox), speaks to the rest of his squad. They have been involved in the abuse of a young Vietnamese girl, which Eriksson refused to take part in. This is what he says:

> Just because each of us might at any second be blown away, we're acting like we can do anything we want, as though it doesn't matter what we do. I'm thinking it's just the opposite. Because we might be dead in the next split-second, maybe we gotta be extra careful what we do. Because maybe it matters more. Maybe it matters more than we ever know.[1]

He's right. It matters because 'it is appointed for man to die once, and after that comes judgement' (Heb. 9:27)—although there is always the chance that the day of the Lord might arrive first, before the day of our death.

But is the day of the Lord 'near'? How is it that Christians have been preaching for nearly two millennia that Jesus' return is at hand? Were the early disciples, as many critics of Christianity claim, mistaken about this? Some go so far as to say that Jesus was deluded when he spoke of his return. Peter gives us a partial answer when he explains that 'with the Lord one day is as a thousand years, and a thousand years as one day' (2 Peter 3:8). Time looks very different to us from how it looks to 'the eternal God' (Deut. 33:27). A further explanation concerns the meaning of the word 'near'. Perhaps translating the word as 'imminent' would be better. The idea is that his return *could* happen at any moment, rather than that it *will* happen within a particular period of time. We need to be poised, to be ready. The parable of the ten virgins (Matt. 25:1–13) warns us that we need to remain on the lookout. While the Lord Jesus does mention a couple of things that have to happen before his return, it would be dangerous to think that we know exactly what constitutes a fulfilment of those conditions. After all, Jesus made it very clear that his second coming will take many people by surprise. If we have our own particular idea of what needs to happen *before* we get ready, and we are mistaken, then we could be among those who are caught out.

Why should Edom have behaved differently? Because the strictness of the judgement they eventually faced would be determined by their treatment of others: 'As you have done, it shall be done to you.' Jesus said, 'with the measure you use it will be measured to you' (Matt. 7:2). The merciless needn't expect mercy from the Lord on the last day. If we don't live our lives according to the golden rule, we'll find that a very different rule operates before the judgement seat of Christ—a rule of strict justice. There will be no cause for complaint; we will have to acknowledge with Adoni-Bezek,

> The merciless needn't expect mercy from the Lord on the last day.

'As I have done, so God has repaid me' (Judg. 1:7). We will be in the position of the suspicious baker who thought he was being cheated by a local farmer. Convinced that the farmer's pounds of butter were lighter than claimed, he had him arrested for fraud. At the trial came the following exchange:

Judge: 'I presume you have scales?'

Farmer: 'Yes, of course, your Honour.'

Judge: 'And weights?'

Farmer: 'No, I don't have a set of weights.'

Judge: 'Then how do you hope to weigh accurately the butter you sell to your neighbour?'

Farmer: 'That's easy. When the baker began to buy from me, I decided to buy my bread from him. I've been using his one-pound loaves to balance my scales. If the weight of the butter is wrong, he has only himself to blame.'[2]

Why should Edom have behaved differently? Because we will be held accountable for our deeds—all of them: 'your deeds shall return on your own head' (v. 15). 'We must all appear before the judgment seat of Christ, so that each one may receive what is due for what he has done in the body, whether good or evil' (2 Cor. 5:10). From our present perspective, judgement for some will seem very much *overdue*.

Some years ago, the sports world was shocked to hear about allegations of drug-taking by a world-renowned cyclist. It was several years after his retirement, and even though many others in his sport had been exposed as drug cheats, he had maintained his innocence. He was eventually stripped of numerous titles and had to pay back huge amounts of money. It took a while, but his sins eventually caught up with him.

In another example, a number of serious charges came to light against a TV celebrity about a year after his death. It gradually became clear that he had successfully kept crimes that stretched across decades secret right up to the day he died. Moral outrage was widespread, and all the fiercer because he could not be called to account for his actions. Only his memory and reputation were affected. Did he get away with it? Did he escape? No; 'each of us will give an account of himself to God' (Rom. 14:12).

A cup of wrath (v. 16)

Edom's deeds, we have been told, are going to return on their own head. Verse 16 makes it clear that Obadiah has a particular deed in mind: they had toasted the fall of Jerusalem—maybe literally, but certainly in their hearts. Ezekiel echoes the words of Obadiah but drops the imagery: 'As you rejoiced over the inheritance of the house of Israel, because it was desolate, so I will deal with you; you shall be desolate' (Ezek. 35:15). Revenge had been sweet, but that was not the end of their ancient enemy. Another scene or two remained to be played out between the old adversaries, and it would involve a reversal of fortunes. The cup of celebration that Edom was revelling in would soon have to be exchanged for one with a distinctly sobering effect. They would not be drinking alone. It would be a shared cup, a cup for all nations—but that would be cold comfort. This would be a cup that they would be stuck with. There would be no further twists and turns of providence ahead, no eventual return to celebration. This cup would be no champagne flute—more of a poisoned chalice.

The imagery of drinking an unwelcome cup crops up a number of times in Scripture. In one of Asaph's psalms he talks about a cup 'in the hand of the LORD' (Ps. 75:8) which God pours out, 'and all the wicked of the earth shall drain it down to the dregs'. It's a cup of judgement. Isaiah and Jeremiah also talk about this cup, but they emphasize that it's a cup of wrath (Isa. 51:17–22; Jer. 25:15, 17, 28; 49:12). Habakkuk speaks of the same cup, but for him it's a cup of shame (Hab. 2:16), while Ezekiel describes 'a cup of horror and desolation' (Ezek. 23:32–34). There would be no delicate sipping of this cup—it would have to be drained down to the dregs. Isaiah has another name for this cup: 'the cup of staggering' (Isa. 51:22).

All of the foreboding and dread that this image conveys becomes even more concentrated, reaching a new level of intensity, as we move into the New Testament and arrive in the garden of Gethsemane. Even the Lord Jesus shrank from drinking this cup. 'My soul is very sorrowful, even to death' were his words just before he said to his Father, 'if it be possible, let this cup pass from me; nevertheless, not as I will, but as you will' (Matt. 26:38–39). We owe everything to that 'nevertheless'. His actual drinking of the cup corresponded with the three hours of darkness as he hung on the cross, and culminated with the cry, 'My God, my God, why have you forsaken me?'[3] We can supply the answer: 'So that all those who believe in you will never have to drink the cup of wrath.'

Death and the curse were in our cup;
O Christ, 'twas full for Thee!
But Thou hast drain'd the last dark drop:
'Tis empty now for me.
That bitter cup, love drank it up;
Now blessings flow for me.[4]

Christ's sufferings mean that we can partake of a different cup altogether. With the psalmist we can now say, 'I will lift up'—not the cup of desolation, but—'the cup of salvation and call on the name of the LORD' (Ps. 116:13). Instead of a cup of horror, Paul tells us that we are now able to share a 'cup of blessing' which is 'a participation in the blood of Christ' (1 Cor. 10:16).

Once they have drained the bitter cup the nations will be forgotten—'as though they had never been'; while those of us who are part of the new covenant (of which the cup is a sign, 1 Cor. 11:25) will drink 'in remembrance of [Christ] … until he comes' (1 Cor. 11:25–26).

For further study ▶

1. Read Romans 2:1–5. What do you think Paul is thinking of when he refers to God's kindness, forbearance and patience? Does he have a specific example or situation in mind?

2. Read 2 Corinthians 3:4–5:15. What kept Paul going in his ministry?

3. Read 2 Timothy 4:1–8, 16–18. What in these verses might help keep Timothy faithful?

4. Read Matthew 25:1–13. What are we to make of the foolish virgins? What kind of people in the church of Christ do they represent?

TO THINK ABOUT AND DISCUSS

1. Can you think of a situation where your actions have been directly influenced by thoughts of future consequences?

2. Have you ever got away with something you know you shouldn't have done? What effect did it have on you?

3. What steps can we take to ensure that we remain watchful? What should this watching involve?

4. How often do you think about the day of judgement? Do you think it would change the way you live if you thought about it more?

7 The day of the Lord for the house of Jacob

(vv. 17–20)

Possession of the land had been the goal of Israel's wanderings in the wilderness. Now Obadiah tells us that on the day of the Lord that goal will finally be reached. Israel's escape will be an escape to holiness and to victory.

Zion's deliverance (and ours) (v. 17)

There is no escape for the men from Mount Esau (vv. 8–9, 18), but on Mount Zion it is a different story. Back in verse 14 we saw Edom cutting off Jerusalem's fugitives (or 'escapees') and handing over its survivors. Now we learn that, despite Edom's best (or worst) efforts, 'there *shall be* those who escape' in Mount Zion (emphasis mine).

When God judges his people he always leaves survivors, sometimes referred to as a 'remnant'. It has been his way of working from the book of Genesis onwards. His dealings with Jacob and his sons had a purpose, as Joseph was able to see (eventually!): 'God sent me before you to preserve for you a remnant on earth, and to keep alive for you many survivors' (Gen. 45:7). It's a purpose that covers the entire Old Testament. When Jerusalem was besieged by Sennacherib's army the prophet Isaiah reassured the people that beyond the judgement 'the surviving remnant of the house of Judah shall again take root downwards and bear fruit upwards. For out of Jerusalem shall go a remnant, and out of Mount Zion a band of survivors' (2 Kings 19:30–31; see also Isa. 4:2; 37:31–32). Ezekiel, having warned Jerusalem of the severity of the judgement it faced (not just a siege, but 'judgment, sword, famine, wild beasts, and pestilence'), also consoled them with the promise that 'some survivors will be left in it' (Ezek. 14:21–22). After the captivity that Isaiah and Ezekiel both predicted Ezra recognized that those who returned with him to Jerusalem were a fulfilment of those earlier promises. The Lord *had* left 'a remnant' and given his people 'a little reviving' (Ezra 9:8; see also 9:13, 15). The message is straightforward: the judgements God brings upon his people always leave a remnant; there will always be those who escape to populate Mount Zion.

If you're a Christian, you may not realize it but you have come to Mount Zion. The writer of Hebrews says so (Heb. 12:22). What does he mean? He helps explain by adding that it is not the earthly Jerusalem that he is referring to, but 'the heavenly Jerusalem'. The deliverance of the literal Mount Zion was a picture, a foreshadowing, of a more complete spiritual deliverance which finds its fulfilment in

Jesus. As with the kingdom of God, there is a sense in which we already came to Zion, spiritually speaking, when we believed. At that point we joined the people of God. But we are also 'looking forward to the city' (Heb. 11:10) whose future arrival we see described in the book of Revelation. There is a 'now' and a 'not yet' aspect to Zion, just as there is when we talk about the kingdom of God. That's why the writer of Hebrews can say that those who have come to Mount Zion have come to 'the spirits of the righteous made perfect, and to Jesus' (Heb. 12:23–24). We have joined them in principle, we're part of the same club, but we're still waiting to meet up with them. The picture in Hebrews anticipates John's vision in Revelation, where he sees 'Mount Zion', and standing on it 'the Lamb' along with his redeemed followers (Rev. 14:1, 3–4). Together at last!

Not only have we come to Zion, but we are also escapees. The writer of Hebrews had warned earlier about the importance of paying attention to the message of salvation, to ensure that his readers would be among those who 'escape' (Heb. 2:3). Then, immediately after the passage about coming to Mount Zion, comes a further warning about the danger of failing to escape (Heb. 12:25). The Lord Jesus warned the scribes and Pharisees of the need to 'escape being sentenced to hell' (Matt. 23:33). Peter tells us that Christians have already, in one sense, 'escaped from the corruption that is in the world' (2 Peter 1:4) but are also, in another sense, in the process of 'escaping from those who live in error' (2 Peter 2:18). Only when we are with the Lord Jesus will the great escape be complete.

While the book of Obadiah is not quoted in the New

Testament, a passage with close links to it is. Part of Joel 2:32 is almost a word-for-word quote[1] from Obadiah 17:

And it shall come to pass that everyone who calls on the name of the LORD shall be saved. **For in Mount Zion and in Jerusalem there shall be those who escape,** as the LORD has said, and among the survivors shall be those whom the LORD calls. (Joel 2:32)	**But in Mount Zion there shall be those who escape,** and it shall be holy, and the house of Jacob shall possess their own possessions. (Obad. 17)

That makes it tremendously significant when Paul quotes the opening clause of Joel 2:32 in Romans (10:13), and when Peter quotes the immediately preceding four verses as well (Acts 2:17–21). It shows that we are not on a flight of fancy when we claim that Obadiah is prophesying New Testament blessings in Old Testament terms. Peter was clear that the events of Pentecost were 'what was uttered through the prophet Joel' (Acts 2:16), and Paul saw ongoing fulfilment as the gospel spread to Gentiles who 'call[ed] on the name of the Lord' (Rom. 10:13). So seeing Obadiah's 'Mount Zion' as ultimately looking forward to John's 'new Jerusalem' (Rev. 3:12; 21:2, 10), and the escapees as Christians who have been delivered 'from the present evil age' (Gal. 1:4), is more than plausible: it's biblical.

Zion's holiness (and ours) (v. 17)

For this remnant it's not a case of simply escaping destruction and of life then getting back to normal; Mount Zion is going to be a different place altogether. It will be transformed. In a word, it will be 'holy', just as the Lord had always planned.

There are two stages in the Lord's plan of redemption: deliverance from, and deliverance to; out of Egypt, and into the promised land. No sooner had Moses and the people crossed the Red Sea than they were praising the Lord, confident that, having brought them through the waters, he would get them safely to his 'holy abode' (Exod. 15:13) and 'plant them on [his] own mountain' (Exod. 15:17). It was a journey from sin to holiness. A place of holiness was the goal—but that meant that his people needed to be made holy en route. Part of his purpose in sending judgement while preserving a remnant was that his people might learn from their mistakes: 'In that day the remnant of Israel and the survivors of the house of Jacob will no more lean on him who struck them, but will lean on the LORD, the Holy One of Israel, in truth' (Isa. 10:20). Ezekiel tells us of how 'those ... who escape will remember [the LORD] among the nations where they are carried captive' (Ezek. 6:9). So the judgements they encounter have a purifying effect on the Lord's people.

> It was a journey from sin to holiness. A place of holiness was the goal—but that meant that his people needed to be made holy en route.

Jesus forgave sinners freely, but twice stressed that holiness should now be their goal: 'From now on sin no more' was how he put it (John 8:11; see also 5:14). The Greek word lying behind the words 'sanctify' and 'holy' in our English

Bibles has the meaning 'to be set apart for God' (see 2 Tim. 2:21), making it clear that Christians have been set apart by God in order that they might be set apart in their lives—set apart from sin and from the world. Our hope as Christians is that one day we will be holy. Our aim as Christians is to be increasingly holy in our daily lives. We are to be 'bringing holiness to completion in the fear of God' (2 Cor. 7:1). It's what the Lord chose us for (Eph. 1:4). It's what the Lord calls us to (1 Thes. 4:7; 2 Tim. 1:9; 1 Peter 1:15). It's what our 'new self' is supposed to be (Eph. 4:24), and what we ought to be (2 Peter 3:11). Holiness, in measure, is not an optional extra in the Christian life; it is an absolute essential (Heb. 12:14). And then holiness in perfection (beyond this life) is, for the Christian, an absolute promise (Eph. 5:27).

Zion's victory (and ours) (v. 18)

The escape of the people and the purifying of the city mark a victory, and that will mean defeat for someone else. The victory of the 'house of Jacob' will be at the expense of the 'house of Esau'. Edom will be left with 'no survivor'. There will be a remnant of God's people, but not of their enemies.

The Lord had given his people many decisive victories before, many of them notable for having left their enemies with no survivors. The two victories granted to Israel as they approached the promised land—against Og and Sihon—were seen as a kind of faith-strengthening example of what God was promising to do for his people as they entered Canaan. The outcomes of the battles were described in the same way to stress the completeness of the victory. And when

Joshua spearheaded the campaign into Canaan itself it was the same story:

- Against Og: 'no survivor left' (Num. 21:35);
- Against Sihon: 'no survivors' (Deut. 2:34);
- At Ai: 'none that survived or escaped' (Josh. 8:22);
- In southern Canaan: 'left none remaining' (Josh. 10:33).

The victories God gives his people are complete—so complete that his people will be a reunited, as well as a victorious, people (i.e. including the 'house of Joseph', Obad. 18); and so complete that their enemies will be like 'stubble' in the path of a raging fire.

John the Baptist used the same imagery to depict the work of the Messiah: the Lord Jesus would baptize his people 'with the Holy Spirit and fire' (Matt. 3:11). Others, though, are described as 'chaff' which he would 'burn with unquenchable fire' (Matt. 3:12). The Lord Jesus said of himself, 'I came to cast fire on the earth, and would that it were already kindled!' (Luke 12:49). On the day of Pentecost the Lord Jesus poured out his Spirit on the church, and we read that 'tongues as of fire ... rested on each one of them' (Acts 2:3). From that point the gospel began to spread like wildfire. Paul described the progress of the gospel as a victory procession:

> thanks be to God, who in Christ always leads us in triumphal procession, and through us spreads the fragrance of the knowledge of him everywhere. For we are the aroma of Christ to God among those who are being saved and among those who are perishing, to one a fragrance from death to death, to the other a fragrance from life to life (2 Cor. 2:14–16).

The difference in fortunes between Edom and Israel is the

same as that between the saved and the unsaved. One day the victory will be complete; our great enemy, the devil, will be 'thrown into the lake of fire' (Rev. 20:10); and we shall be 'more than conquerors through him who loved us' (Rom. 8:37).

Zion's inheritance (and ours) (vv. 17, 19–20)

The phrase 'and the house of Jacob shall possess their own possessions' (v. 17) brings us to another future blessing that Israel will enjoy. The Hebrew could be translated in any one of three ways, the final choice depending on the context. It could indeed be, as the text reads, 'possess their ... possessions', but the alternatives are 'dispossess their dispossessors' and 'inherit their inheritance'. It may be that the ambiguity is deliberate. Actually, all three readings work in the context and make much the same point: Israel will recover land that they had lost to their enemies, and acquire more besides.

Possession of the land to its full extent had been often promised but never realized in Israel's eventful history. When Obadiah says that the time will come when 'the house of Jacob will possess their ... possessions', he might well have been tempted to add the words 'and not before time!' Roughly fifteen hundred years earlier the Lord had promised Abram, 'I am the LORD who brought you out from Ur of the Chaldeans to give you this land to possess' (Gen. 15:7). There was also the promise given to Moses that the Lord would drive the Canaanites out 'little by little' until they had possessed the land (Exod. 23:30). It was a promise believed by Caleb and Joshua (Num. 14:24)—but only by Caleb and

Joshua. Unbelief on the part of the people meant forty years in the wilderness, but at the end of their wanderings the promise was repeated (Num. 33:53)—again and again (Deut. 1:39; 5:31, 33; 6:1; 10:11; 11:8, 31; 12:1; 15:4; 17:14; 19:2, 14; 21:1; 25:19)! Along with the promise came an exhortation to 'take possession' (Deut. 1:21; 2:24, 31; 4:1, 22; 11:8, 31). As someone has pointed out, the promises were supposed to be stimulants, not sedatives, and that's how they worked on Joshua. All went well as Joshua led the people into the promised land. Joshua 'left nothing undone of all that the LORD had commanded Moses' (Josh. 11:15), and 'not one word … failed of all the good things that the LORD … promised' either (23:14). There was just one problem: with Joshua's work all but done, 'there remain[ed] yet very much land to possess' (13:1). The close of the book of Joshua and the opening of the book of Judges have as their theme Israel's failure to possess the land in full. And down through their history, even under Solomon, they never occupied the full extent of the land that the Lord had given them, and it was entirely their fault. One day, though—Obadiah tells us—it will be a different story.

Verses 19–20 are like the plotting of troops' progress on a table in the war room. It is the antidote to the many reports at the end of Joshua of how various tribes failed to possess their portion of the land. Finally things will be put right. The places mentioned give us a geography lesson. Mount Esau is, unsurprisingly, top of the hit list—on the south-east edge of Israel's territory. The Philistines are to the west, Ephraim and Samaria to the north, and Gilead to the east. Zarephath is to the north-west, and the Negeb lies to the south. We are being told that Israel will expand in all directions to fill the entire land that should have been theirs long before. The people mentioned tell us something else: 'those of the Negeb', 'those of the Shephelah', 'Benjamin', and then two groups of exiles are returning even as Israel is expanding. Some of this expansion was achieved in the days of the Maccabbees, but by no means all.

That was then, but this is now. What does all this have to do with us? Again, we are part of the fulfilment of this prophecy. The book of Acts charts the progress of the gospel, beginning in Jerusalem and then expanding to 'Judea and Samaria, and to the end of the earth' (Acts 1:8). It's still spreading.

> Just as we are told that human beings use only a small fraction of their brain, so we fail to realize our full potential as Christians.

There is a more personal application to us of the phrase 'possess their own possessions' (v. 17). We have a promise that the church and Christians will one day be saved in the fullest sense (that of final deliverance and victory), but there is also a process of 'working out' our salvation in the present that we are responsible for (see Phil. 2:12). Will we participate in the spread of the gospel? And will we 'possess our possessions' in the here and now? That is to say, will we avail ourselves of all that can be ours in Christ? Just as we are told that human beings use only a small fraction of their brain, and just as the computer I am using to type this book is capable of far more than I ever ask of it—so we fail to realize our full potential as Christians. We often resemble the former slave of a southern plantation-owner in America. As a reward for his faithfulness his master left him $50,000 in his will, an enormous sum in those days. The lawyer responsible for administering the dead man's estate duly informed the man of the vast amount that had been deposited at the local bank. When weeks passed without the money being touched, the bank manager called in the former slave and again explained to him how much he was now worth. The former slave's reply was a simple one: 'Sir, do you think I could have fifty cents to buy a sack of cornmeal?' Having never handled money before, the man had no comprehension of his wealth. Do we really have a proper grasp of what constitute 'the unsearchable riches of Christ' (Eph. 3:8) and of what it means to 'be filled with the Spirit' (Eph. 5:18)? Have we done any more than scratch the surface when it comes to the treasure that the Scriptures contain? Don't we feel the continuing need to join with the disciple in asking, 'Lord, teach us to pray' (Luke 11:1)?

For every Christian and every church, 'there remains yet very much land to possess' (Josh. 13:1).

For further study ▶

1. Read Amos 9:11–12 and Acts 15. How does the quoting of Amos in Acts support the view that the book of Obadiah finds fulfilment in the spread of the gospel?
2. Read Romans 9:22–29 and 11:1–5. How did Paul apply the Old Testament idea of a remnant to what was happening in the early church?
3. Read Hebrews 2:1–4 and 12:25–29. What do we need to do to guard against the danger of failing to escape?

TO THINK ABOUT AND DISCUSS

1. What kind of discipline from the Lord can help us on the way to holiness, and how?
2. What sorts of victories can we realistically expect in this life as Christians?
3. What do you think your particular contribution to the spread of the gospel is supposed to be, and how are you getting on?
4. Which areas of the Christian life do you feel you have failed to explore fully to date, and what can you do about it?

8 The kingship of the Lord

(v. 21)

Back in the days of the judges the Lord had raised up deliverers when his people needed them. In Obadiah's day of the Lord it will be no different. The leaders Israel needs will be supplied— initially to save, and then to rule. There will be many leaders, but only one king: a king for whom only an everlasting kingdom will do.

Saviours

Much of Obadiah has been about judgement because it is a prophecy 'concerning Edom' (v. 1) and the land of Mount Esau. The Lord's purposes for *his* people and *his* mount, however, end in salvation. There had been numerous deliverances throughout Israel's history and another one was on its way. Each time the Lord came to the rescue he raised up a 'saviour' to do the rescuing. The Hebrew word translated 'saviours' is a root from which the name Joshua (literally, 'the Lord saves') comes. After living up to his name, Joshua was followed by a generation 'who did not know the LORD' and who 'did what was evil in the sight of the LORD' (Judg. 2:10–11). In anger the Lord 'sold them into the hand of their surrounding enemies' (2:14). But this is a God who 'in wrath remember[s] mercy' (Hab. 3:2), and so he 'raised up judges, who saved them out of the hand of those who plundered them' (Judg. 2:16). The verb 'save' here shares the same root as the term 'saviour' and is used of Othniel, Ehud, Shamgar, Tola and Samson, making it clear that 'saving' was pretty much a job description when it came to the judges (Judg. 3:9, 15, 31; 10:1; 13:5; see also Neh. 9:27). It was no different when it came to Israel's kings, as we find that Saul, David and Jehoahaz did their fair share of 'saving' too (1 Sam. 9:16; 23:2; 2 Kings 13:5).

Obadiah may have been prophesying primarily of the 'saviours' raised up to encourage those who returned to Jerusalem after the captivity in the work of rebuilding—men such as Zerubbabel, Ezra and Nehemiah, along with the prophets Haggai and Zechariah. He could even have been looking forward to the time between the Testaments and the exploits of Judas Maccabaeus and later John Hyrcanus.

Be that as it may, the ultimate fulfilment is to be found in one called 'Jesus' (a Greek form of Joshua) because 'he will save his people from their sins' (Matt. 1:21). Although Jesus is *the* Saviour in a unique way, the list doesn't end there. Peter, Paul, John, Apollos and Timothy, in their own way, were also used by God to bring salvation to many. Augustine, Wycliffe, Luther, Calvin, Wesley, Whitefield, Spurgeon—names continue to be added. One day the list will come to an end, with the return of *the* Saviour. In the meantime, we are assured that the church and each Christian will have all the 'saviours' and 'salvations' they need. You may be able to look back and see how the Lord 'raised up' certain people in your own life to 'save you' from a life that would have led to destruction, from a foolish course of action, a period of backsliding or an unwise decision. Maybe in his providence he worked a mini-salvation which didn't involve anyone else. Whatever our own experience, as Christians we can share Paul's confidence that 'the Lord will rescue me from every evil deed and bring me safely into his heavenly kingdom' (2 Tim. 4:18).

> You may be able to look back and see how the Lord 'raised up' certain people in your own life to 'save you' from a life that would have led to destruction.

Mount Zion

We have already seen Mount Zion as the place of escape and a place of holiness. It was the centre of David's kingdom and became the home of the ark, making it a spiritual focal point for worship too. Bringing the ark of the covenant to Mount Zion wasn't simply David's idea. The psalmist tells us that the Lord chose it 'for his dwelling place' (Ps. 132:13). Many of the psalms speak about it in those terms (Ps. 9:11; 84:7; 99:2), and Jerusalem benefited from the protection of its 'great King' (Ps. 48:2). Zion is also viewed, poetically, as the source of blessing and help (Ps. 14:7; 20:2; 50:2; 53:6; 110:2;

128:5; 134:3). But it's not just the name of a place; it is also used as a name for a people—literally, for the inhabitants of Jerusalem; poetically, for the people of God.

Zion had a role in prophecy as well as poetry. Isaiah had a vision of what would 'come to pass in the latter days', and it involved 'the mountain of the house of the LORD' (Isa. 2:2). Somehow it is transformed into 'the highest of the mountains' and it attracts 'all the nations' to it, no longer the centre of David's rule but of world rule (2:3–4). This is a very different Zion from the one we're familiar with. This Zion is to be made 'majestic for ever, a joy from age to age' (Isa. 60:15). The following verses establish that Isaiah's vision is one that merges with the apostle John's. He, too, saw the glory of God giving light to the city (Isa. 60:19–20; Rev. 21:23–24). This new Jerusalem will be the centre of the new heaven and earth which heralds the fulfilment of all the covenant promises, summed up in the words, 'Behold, the dwelling place of God is with man' (Rev. 21:3).

Rulers

The Hebrew word translated 'rule' here could equally have been translated 'judge' (as it usually is in the Old Testament). It's what Moses, the judges, Samuel and Solomon did in governing the people of Israel. It's also what the Lord Jesus stressed that he *hadn't* come to do during his earthly ministry (John 12:47). His second coming, though, *will* be to judge the earth (1 Chr. 16:33; Ps. 96:13; 98:9).

Here in Obadiah, salvation and victory having been accomplished, the Lord's people find themselves ruling over their enemies on Mount Esau. It's yet another image of final deliverance that is taken up in the New Testament. In the parable of the ten minas, Jesus speaks of the nobleman who, having received a kingdom, rewards his servants with authority over cities (Luke 19:17–19). That tallies with the picture here at the end of Obadiah and with the teaching of the apostle Paul. Paul asked the Christians in Corinth, 'do you not know that the saints will judge the world?' (1 Cor. 6:2). It is a tantalizing comment because it is teaching that is not spelled out in detail elsewhere in the New Testament, though we have another reference, in Revelation 20:4, that speaks of 'those to whom the authority to judge was committed' and of others who 'reigned with Christ'. I can't claim fully to have grasped how all this fits chronologically in Revelation's description of the end times or how exactly it will work when the time comes, but the teaching is there all the same. We can look forward to a 'judging/ruling' role of some sort, which is part of the final victory of God's people and the establishment of an everlasting kingdom.

King

While his disciples will rule, the rule that they exercise will be that of deputies. The kingship (the Hebrew word in v. 21 should really be translated 'kingship' rather than 'kingdom') of this kingdom is the Lord's. Israel's history could be summed up as a series of let-downs as far as their earthly kingship was concerned. The first king had been a disappointment, David's reign was marred by moral failure, and even Solomon's glorious reign ended in apostasy. Then came the search for a worthy successor—the new 'David' that had been promised. Asa began well, but finished badly;

Jehoshaphat stood out, but made bad alliances; Uzziah and Hezekiah had pride issues; and good King Josiah made a bad decision that brought his reign to a premature end. Jotham is the only king of whom the Bible has nothing bad to say, and yet it is made clear that the people in his day were idolatrous, despite his best efforts to bring them back to God. By now, in Obadiah's day, after all those false dawns, it appeared as though the sun had set on any hopes of the great king and kingdom Israel looked forward to. After the fall of Jerusalem to the Babylonians there was no king and there was no kingdom. But, in a way, that must have made a promise like this gleam and glisten all the more brightly in the darkness.

Obadiah is presenting his picture of God's final triumph in terms that the people of his day could understand, but it is the same scene that many others glimpsed in prophetic vision or heard in divine promise. David, though king himself, was in no doubt that 'kingship belongs to the LORD, and he rules over the nations' (Ps. 22:28). The reality of that rule will not be clear until the final victory, the day that Micah knew was coming, when 'the LORD will reign over them in Mount Zion from this time forth and for evermore' (Micah 4:7).

The apostle John saw the exact moment when 'the kingdom of the world [will] become the kingdom of our Lord and of his Christ' (Rev. 11:15), but Daniel had seen it long before: 'one like a son of man ... was given dominion and glory and a kingdom, that all peoples, nations, and languages should serve him; his dominion is an everlasting dominion, which shall not pass away, and his kingdom one that shall not be destroyed' (Dan. 7:13–14). What a kingdom it will be! John struggles for words to portray the glory he sees. He even struggles for pictures to convey the reality of what will be. The people of the kingdom will spend all eternity amazed at the inheritance that is finally theirs.

The story so far ...

The story of Obadiah is the story of Israel throughout the Old Testament: mockery and judgement at the hand of their enemies, followed by vindication and victory over those same foes.

The story of Obadiah is also the story of the Saviour. Those who were related to him and should have been on his side joined forces with his enemies, aiming to humiliate and then destroy him. Their deeds caught up with them some forty years later, as Jerusalem was razed to the ground (in AD 70). Meanwhile, Jesus 'escaped' from the grave and inherited a people (Ps. 2:8) and a kingdom.

The story of Obadiah is also the story of the church. The jump from Israel and Edom to the New Testament church and its enemies is not a leap in the dark: it has biblical support from Luke's account of the council of Jerusalem, in the book of Acts. There James quotes a passage from the Old Testament prophet Amos which, in the Hebrew original, refers to Edom. James said that the time of restoration which Amos described was finding fulfilment in the response of the Gentiles to the gospel. Things get a bit complicated because James was quoting a Greek translation of the Old Testament which refers to 'mankind' rather than 'Edom', but the application is clear enough.

The story of Obadiah is our story as individual believers too. Our Saviour has warned us that others will 'revile [us] and persecute [us]' (Matt. 5:11). We must first suffer with our Saviour if we are to be glorified with him. We are to 'share his sufferings' before experiencing 'the power of his resurrection' (Phil. 3:10). It is 'through many tribulations' that we must go, and only then will we properly 'enter the kingdom of God' (Acts 14:22). But we will get there in the end. The conclusion of Obadiah is also the conclusion of history and the beginning of eternity. The kingdom, in answer to our prayers, will have finally come.

FOR FURTHER STUDY

1. Read 1 Samuel 25:23–34 and 2 Samuel 12:1–13. How might David have viewed Abigail and Nathan as 'saviours'? In what ways are they similar, and how do they differ?

2. Read Psalm 48 and the words of John Newton's hymn 'Glorious Things of Thee Are Spoken'. How does Newton interpret this psalm? Are there any details of the psalm that can be applied to the New Testament church? If so, how?

3. Read 2 Thessalonians 1:4–10. How many elements of Obadiah's prophecy can you identify in these verses?

TO THINK ABOUT AND DISCUSS

1. What 'saviours' and 'salvations' can you identify in your own life?

2. What have you generally thought you've been asking for when you have prayed, 'Thy kingdom come'?

3. In what ways can the kingdom come in this present age?

Endnotes

Chapter 1

1 *The Works of George Whitefield: Journals* (Oswestry: Quinta Press, 2000), p. 20; available at www.quintapress.com/files/whitefield/Journals.pdf.

2 Interestingly, Peter, in his first letter, uses military language along these lines when he says that 'God opposes [sets himself in battle array against] the proud' (1 Peter 5:5).

3 I think there are good reasons to prefer the NIV 1984 rendering of Hebrews 12:17, 'He [Esau] could bring about no change of mind.' It is true to the Greek and better fits the Old Testament context (Gen. 27:34, 38), which tells of Esau trying to get his father to reconsider (i.e. change his mind, or 'repent').

Chapter 4

1 As mentioned in the Introduction, Herod was an Idumaean—the name, in Jesus' day, used to describe those from the region of ancient Edom.

2 Popularly attributed to Napoleon, though I have been unable to trace the original source.

Chapter 5

1 The Edomites were driven from their own land by Nabatean Arabs in about 312 BC. Though their existence as a people group persisted into New Testament times, they fade from history after the fall of Jerusalem in AD 70.

2 Traditionally attributed to Burke, though I have been unable to trace the original source.

3 James Ussher (1581–1656) was Archbishop of Armagh and Primate of All Ireland.

4 Quoted by J. C. Ryle, *Holiness* (WORDsearch edn, 2004), ch. 1.

5 The full study, carried out in 1973, was published in John M. Darley and C. Daniel Batson, '"From Jerusalem to

Jericho": A Study of Situational and Dispositional Variables in Helping Behavior', *Journal of Personality and Social Psychology* 27, no. 1 (1973), pp. 100–108; it can be found at http://www3.nd.edu/~wcarbona/darley%20and%20batson%20-%20from%20jerusalem%20to%20jericho.pdf.

6   Quoted in Erwin W. Lutzer, *When a Nation Forgets God: 7 Lessons We Must Learn from Nazi Germany* ([Kindle edn] Chicago: Moody Press, 2010), ch. 1.

7   *The Essays of Arthur Schopenhauer: On Human Nature*; at Project Gutenberg, www.gutenberg.org/.

8   This quote appears on a number of websites, but I have been unable to find the source.

9   Whether this will actually happen in reality is disputed, though there is some evidence that if the heating of the water is gradual enough it might. Thankfully, the scientific community has recognized that putting this to the test would be unethical.

10 This could mean 'cut off' as in 'slaughter', but probably, in this context, means 'intercept'.

Chapter 6

1   Edward K. Rowell, *1001 Quotes, Illustrations, and Humorous Stories for Preachers, Teachers, and Writers* (Grand Rapids, MI: Baker, 2005), p. 228.

2   From 'The Cheater Who Cheated Himself', *Preaching Today*, http://www.preachingtoday.com/illustrations/2003/january/14111.html.

3   One could argue that all of Christ's sufferings surrounding the cross were part of the cup. His prayer in Gethsemane establishes that he had not begun to drink the cup at that point. The Gospel narratives certainly concentrate on the cross itself, and the three hours of darkness mark the heart of his sufferings.

4   Anne R. Cousin (1824–1906),
    'O Christ, What Burdens
    Bowed Thy Head'.

Chapter 7

1   That it is a quote is indicated by
    the words 'as the LORD has
    said'.

Further reading

Allen, Leslie C., *The Books of Joel, Obadiah, Jonah and Micah* (New International Commentary on the Old Testament; Grand Rapids, MI: Eerdmans, 1976)

Alexander, T. Desmond, David W. Baker and Bruce Waltke, *Obadiah, Jonah, Micah* (Tyndale Commentary; Nottingham: IVP, 2009)

Bentley, Michael, *Turning Back to God* (Welwyn Commentary; Darlington: Evangelical Press, 2000)

Bridger, Gordon, *The Message of Obadiah, Nahum and Zephaniah* (Bible Speaks Today; Nottingham: IVP, 2010)

Field, David, *Obadiah* (Exploring the Bible; Leominster: Day One, 2008)

Shenton, Tim, *Nahum and Obadiah* (Exploring the Bible; Leominster: Day One, 2007)

Wiersbe, Warren, *Be Concerned* (Minor Prophets) (Colorado Springs, CO: David C. Cook, 2010)